bridges to contemplative living
with thomas merton

lent and holy week

edited by jonathan montaldo & robert g. toth
of the merton institute for contemplative living

ave maria press  notre dame, indiana

Every effort has been made to give proper acknowledgment to authors and copyright holders of the text herein. If any omissions or errors have been made, please notify the publisher, who will correct it in future editions. Ave Maria Press gratefully acknowledges the permission of the following publishers for use of excerpts from these books:

Contemplation in a World of Action by Thomas Merton, copyright © 1973 by the Abbey of Gethsemani. Used by permission of Doubleday, a division of Random House, Inc.

He is Risen by Thomas Merton, copyright © 1975 by Argus Communications. Used by permission.

Humility Matters by Margaret Mary Funk, O.S.B., copyright © 2005 by Continuum Publishing. Used by kind permission.

"Loretto and Gethsemani" by Thomas Merton, copyright © 1962 by The Abbey of Gethsemani. Used with permission.

Merton's Palace of Nowhere, by James Finley, copyright © 1978 by Ave Maria Press. Used by permission.

"The Mission of Orthodoxy," by Alexander Schmemann in *Concern 3*, 1968 reprinted by Conciliar Press, copyright ©1989, 1994. Used by permission of Conciliar Press.

The Monastic Journey by Thomas Merton, edited by Brother Patrick Hart, copyright © 1992 by Cistercian Publications.

The *New Revised Standard Version* (Anglicized Edition), copyright 1989, 1995 by the Division of Christian Education of the National Council of the Churches of Christ in the United States of America. Used by permission. All rights reserved.

One Heart Full of Love by Mother Teresa, edited by José Luis González-Balado, copyright © 1988. Used with permission of St. Anthony Messenger Press.

The Psalms, A New Translation, arranged by Joseph Gelineau, copyright © 1963 by Paulist Press, Inc., New York, Mahwah, NJ. Used with permission. www.paulistpress.com

The Roots of Christian Mysticism by Olivier Clément, copyright © 1993 by New City Press. Used by permission of New City Press.

The Sacrament of Love, translated by Paul Evdokimov, copyright © 2008 by Saint Vladimir's Seminary Press.

Founded in 1865, Ave Maria Press is a ministry of the Indiana Province of Holy Cross.

www.avemariapress.com

ISBN-10 1-59471-204-2   ISBN-13 978-1-59471-204-3

Cover and text design by Andy Wagoner.

Cover image © Robert Hill Photography

Photograph of Thomas Merton on page 7 by John Lyons. Used with permission of the Merton Legacy Trust.

Interior photograph © Jupiter Images Unlimited

Printed and bound in the United States of America.

It is necessary that, at the beginning of this fast, the Lord should show Himself to us in His mercy. The purpose of Lent is not only expiation, to satisfy the divine justice, but above all is a preparation to rejoice in His love. And this preparation consists in receiving the gift of His mercy—a gift which we receive insofar as we open our hearts to it, casting out what cannot remain in the same room with mercy.

Now one of the things we must cast out first of all is fear. Fear narrows the little entrance of our heart. It shrinks our capacity to love. It freezes up our power to give ourselves. If we were terrified of God as an inexorable judge, we would not confidently await His mercy, or approach Him trustfully in prayer. Our peace and our joy in Lent are a guarantee of grace.

THOMAS MERTON
SEASONS OF CELEBRATION

A NOTE ABOUT INCLUSIVE LANGUAGE

Merton wrote at a time before inclusive language was common practice. In light of his inclusive position on so many issues and his references to our essential unity, we hope these texts will be read from an inclusive point of view.

CONTENTS

INTRODUCTION

WHAT DO WE MEAN BY CONTEMPLATIVE LIVING?

Life is a spiritual journey. Contemplative living is a way of responding to our everyday experiences by consciously attending to our relationships. It deepens our awareness of our connectedness and communion with others, becomes a positive force of change in our lives, and provides meaningful direction to our journey. Ultimately, contemplative living leads us to a sense of well-being, profound gratitude, and a clearer understanding of our purpose in life.

Living contemplatively begins with ourselves but leads us in the end to embrace deeply not only our truest self, but God, neighbor, and all of creation. By reflecting on our everyday experiences, we seek the depths of our inner truth. By exploring our beliefs, illusions, attitudes, and assumptions, we find our true self and discover how we relate to the larger community. Contemplative living directs our minds and hearts to the truly important issues of human existence, making us less likely to be captivated by the superficial distractions that so easily occupy our time.

WHO WAS THOMAS MERTON?

For over sixty years, the thought and writings of Thomas Merton have guided spiritual seekers across the world. His writings offer important insights into four essential relationships—with self, with God, with other people, and with all of creation. While the Christian tradition was the foundation of his perspective, he was open and inclusive in his examination of other religious traditions, recognizing the important contribution of all faith traditions to the history of civilization. He drew from their strengths to enhance the spiritual growth of individuals and communities.

Thomas Merton was born in Prades, France, in 1915. His mother was from the United States and his father from New Zealand. Educated in France, England, and the United States, he received a master's degree in English from Columbia University. In 1938 he was baptized into the Catholic Church. He taught at St. Bonaventure University for a year and then in 1941 entered the Cistercian Order as a monk of the Abbey of Gethsemani in Kentucky. Directed by his Abbot, Dom Frederic Dunne, Merton wrote his autobiography, *The Seven Storey Mountain*, which was published in 1948.

For fifteen years he served as Master of Scholastics and Novices while writing many books and articles on the spiritual life, interreligious understanding, peace, and social justice issues. In December of 1968, he journeyed to Asia to attend a conference of contemplatives near Bangkok, Thailand. While there he was accidentally electrocuted and died at the age of fifty-three.

Interest in Merton has grown steadily since his death. *The Seven Storey Mountain*, which appears on lists of the one hundred most important books of the last century, has been in print ever since its first edition and has sold millions of copies. The volume of printed work by and about him attests to Merton's popularity.

His works have been translated into thirty-five languages and new foreign language editions continue to be printed. The International Thomas Merton Society currently has thirty chapters in the United States and fourteen in other countries.

Thomas Merton is distinguished among contemporary spiritual writers by the depth and substance of his thinking. Merton was a scholar who distilled the best thinking of the best theologians, philosophers, and poets throughout the centuries, from both the West and the East, and presented their ideas in the context of the Christian worldview. His remarkable and enduring popularity indicates that his work continues to speak to the minds and hearts of people searching for answers to life's important questions. For many he is a spiritual guide, and for others he offers a place to retreat to in difficult times. His writings take people into deep places within themselves and offer insight into the paradoxes of life. Merton struggled to be a contemplative in a world of action, yet he offered no quick fix or "Ten Easy Steps" to a successful spiritual life.

Using *Bridges to Contemplative Living with Thomas Merton*

Bridges is intended for anyone seeking to live more contemplatively. For some it initiates a spiritual journey, for others it leads to re-examination or recovery of a neglected spiritual life, and for still others it deepens an already vibrant spirituality. Through reflection and dialogue on specific spiritual themes, participants revisit and refresh their perspectives on and understanding of life. They explore the strength and balance of the relationships that ultimately determine who they are: the relationships with self, God, others, and nature. Through examining these relationships, participants probe their understanding of life's great questions:

"Who am I?"

"Who is God?"

"Why am I here?"

"What am I to do with my life?"

The selected readings move participants in and out of four dimensions of contemplative living: *Awakening* to an ever-deepening awareness of "true-self"; *Contemplation* of a life experienced from a God-centered perspective; *Compassion* in relationships with others; and *Unity* realized in our undeniable and essential interconnectedness with all of creation. This fourfold process of spiritual formation frames much of Merton's thought and writing.

This is not a spiritual formation program in some "otherworldly" sense. Merton insisted that our spiritual life is our everyday lived experience. There is no separation between them. *Bridges* does not require an academic background in theology, religion, or spirituality, nor does it require the use of any particular spiritual practices or prayers. There are no levels of perfection, goals to attain, or measurements of progress. This is not an academic or scholarly undertaking. Everyone will find a particular way of contemplative living within his or her own circumstances, religious tradition, and spiritual practices.

The *Bridges to Contemplative Living with Thomas Merton* series is especially designed for small group dialogue. The selected themes of each session are intended to progressively inform and deepen the relationships that form our everyday lives. Each session begins with scripture and ends in prayer. In between there are time and mental space for spiritual reading, reflection, and contemplative dialogue.

WHAT DO WE MEAN BY CONTEMPLATIVE DIALOGUE?

Contemplative dialogue is meant to be non-threatening, a "safe place" for open sharing and discussion. It is not outcome-oriented. It's not even about fully understanding or comprehending what one reads or hears from the other participants. The focus is on *listening* rather than formulating a response to what another is saying. Simply hearing and accepting another's point of view and reflecting on it can inform and enlighten our own perspective in a way that debating or analyzing it cannot. The pace of conversation is slower in contemplative dialogue than in most other conversations. We are challenged to listen more carefully and approach different points of view by looking at the deeper values and issues underlying them.

EIGHT PRINCIPLES FOR ENTERING INTO CONTEMPLATIVE DIALOGUE

1. Keep in mind that *Bridges* focuses on our "lived experience" and how the session theme connects to everyday life. Keep your comments rooted in your own experience and refrain from remarks that are overly abstract, philosophical, or theoretical.

2. Express your own thoughts knowing that others will listen and reflect upon what you say. It is helpful to use "I" statements like "I believe . . ." or "My assumption is that . . ." or "My experience has been. . . ." Others in the group may very well not respond to your thoughts verbally; trust that they are hearing you.

3. Pay attention to the assumptions, attitudes, and experiences underlying your initial or surface thoughts on the topic. Ask yourself questions like: "Why am I drawn to this particular part of the reading?" "What makes me feel this way?"

4. Remember to listen first and refrain from thinking about how you might respond to another's comments. Simply listen to and accept his or her thoughts on the subject without trying to challenge, critique, or even respond aloud to them.

5. Trust the group. Observe how the participants' ideas, reflections, common concerns, assumptions, and attitudes come together and form a collective group mind.

6. Reflect before speaking and be concise. Make one point or relate one experience, then stop and allow others to do the same.

7. Expect periods of silence during the dialogue. Learn to be comfortable with the silence and resist the urge to speak just because there is silence.

8. Avoid cross-talking. In time you will adjust to saying something and not receiving a response and to listening without asking a question, challenging, or responding directly. Simply speaking to the theme or idea from your own experience or perspective takes some practice. Be patient with yourself and the other members of your group and watch for deepening levels of dialogue.

These principles for Contemplative Dialogue are extracted from the work of The Centre for Contemplative Dialogue. For more complete information visit www.contemplativedialogue.org

ADDITIONAL RESOURCES

Online resources available at www.avemariapress.com include:

- Leader's Guide
- Sample pages
- Suggested Retreat Schedule
- Program Evaluation Form
- Links to other books by and about Thomas Merton
- Interview with Robert Toth, executive director of The Merton Institute for Contemplative Living

From the Merton Institute for Contemplative Living: www.mertoninstitute.org

Merton: A Film Biography (1 hour) provides an excellent overview on Merton's life and spiritual journey.

Soul Searching: The Journey of Thomas Merton is a sixty-seven minute DVD that goes to the heart of Merton's spiritual journey through the perspective of Merton's friends, Merton scholars, and authorities on the spiritual life.

Contemplation and Action is a periodic newsletter from The Merton Institute with information about new Merton publications, programs, and events. It is free and can be obtained by visiting the Institute's website or calling 1-800-886-7275.

The Thomas Merton Spiritual Development Program is a basic introduction to Merton's life and his insights on contemplative spirituality, social justice, and inter-religious dialogue. Especially designed for youth, it includes a participant's workbook/journal.

Weekly Merton Reflections Receive a brief reflection from Merton's works via e-mail each week by registering at www.mertoninstitute.org or by contacting:

The Merton Institute for Contemplative Living
2117 Payne Street
Louisville, KY 40206
1-800-886-7275

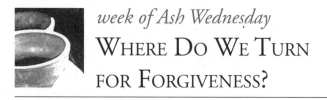

week of Ash Wednesday
WHERE DO WE TURN FOR FORGIVENESS?

OPENING REFLECTION

FROM PSALM 50 IN *THE PSALMS, A NEW TRANSLATION*, ARRANGED BY JOSEPH GELINEAU

> Indeed you love truth in the heart;
> then in the secret of my heart teach me wisdom.
> O purify me, then I shall be clean;
> O wash me, I shall be whiter than snow.
>
> O rescue me, God, my helper,
> and my tongue shall ring out your goodness.
> O Lord, open my lips
> and my mouth shall declare your praise.

INTRODUCTION TO THE TEXTS

No sin is private, hurting no one but ourselves. A secret good deed has public consequences. We are interdependent and social creatures. We are one body. We need one another. Lent provides a perennial occasion to acknowledge and attend to our interrelatedness, to our most intimate and our most universal communities of love and concern.

When Thomas Merton, after visiting his doctor, stepped out on the busy sidewalk at the corner of Fourth and Walnut Streets in downtown Louisville, Kentucky, the illusion of separateness from everyone he saw faded to reveal that "there are no strangers."

He wrote of this epiphany in his journal: "There, there is God in my own Kind, my own Kind—'Kind' which means 'likeness' and which means 'love' and which means 'child.' Mankind. Like one another, the dear 'Kind' of sinners united and embraced in only one heart, in only one Kindness, which is the Heart and Kindness of God" (*A Search for Solitude*, pp. 182–183). Lent is a season for *metanoia*, a change of heart and mind from "former ways of life" that delude us into living as if we could be separate from one another. Lent reeducates us for living communally. Lent calls us to the truth of our unity as we celebrate our being one body in Christ.

MERTON'S VOICE
FROM *SEASONS OF CELEBRATION*

But where shall the sinner turn for pardon? To God, obviously. And the first thing is of course to seek Him in the depths of our heart, asking pardon for our sins. But the Christian conscience, enlightened by the Holy Spirit, tells us that this inner movement of repentance in the privacy of the heart, though it is essential, is not enough by itself. For sin is not a purely individual affair, and neither is pardon. However private it may be, sin remains in some sense everybody's business because everyone is affected by the evil that is in the heart of one. It is not possible for us to live so separated from others, so isolated and private in our own hearts, that our secret selfishness and sin will not affect others. We are involved in each other's lives, not by choice but by necessity, for that is the way we are made. No one can pretend successfully to live purely in his or her own private universe and remain sane. The very condition of normal human life is community, communication, and "conversation" in the old Latin sense of *conversatio*—exchange on the level of social living. The lives of all of us are inextricably mixed together, and the salvation and damnation of souls is involved in this inescapable communication of freedoms. Either we will love and help one another or we will hate and attack one another, in which latter case we will all be one another's hell. . . .

The heart of the Christian message is precisely reconciliation in the Spirit of Love so that communion in freedom turns into communion in beatitude. In which case heaven is communion with "others" (pp. 222–223).

ANOTHER VOICE
MARY MARGARET FUNK, O.S.B., *HUMILITY MATTERS*

In the foundational renunciation signified by baptism, we surrender our false self, generated by our egocentric desires. Since sin is living heedlessly, harming others or ourselves, we renounce these patterns of ignorance and sin by choosing a better way for ourselves and others. Furthermore, we enter into a process of critical discernment not just between good and evil, but regarding the hierarchy of goods. In other words, I renounce not just what may be harmful, but also what may be objectively good in itself, but not good for me. The phrase "former way of life" describes attachment to our family, property as possession, status linked to employment, rank in society, educational, racial, or gender entitlements, and any over-identification with what I do. These attachments dull our zeal and give us a kind of numbness born of unconsciousness toward our real life and the lives of others. . . .

When one renounces one's "former way of life," this life unto death is replaced by an apostolic way of love. We imitate Christ Jesus, as the early disciples are described as doing in the Acts of the Apostles. We see the early Christian community living by new motives, sharing goods in common, mindful of the poor, keeping the gospel as sacred and a way to restore the original order of creation, fulfilling civic duties, and striving to live justly according to the words and deeds of Jesus. Like these early ancestors on the Christian way, we renounce our former way of life precisely to live the gospel life.

But this conversion is difficult to sustain. We get pulled down. We sometimes are ignorant of the good. We are inclined toward evil and thin on resolve. We tend to get weighed down by our human condition—whether the primordial sin of the earliest generations, or the sin of our immediate generations, or our own personal sins. The way out is to return to those baptismal waters and take the plunge again—this time diving deeply into the saving river. Each time we take the plunge and rise again, we commit ourselves to the contemplative or interior way of life. In a sense, taking up the spiritual journey is to live beneath the surface and to stay immersed in those baptismal waters with Christ Jesus and then to rise with him above the water and live as he did (pp. 19–21).

Reflect and Dialogue

What words or sentences in these readings most resonate with your life's experiences?

How has your personal understanding of Lent, sin, and conversion changed as you have matured in your spiritual life?

What hoped-for change in your mind and heart (*metanoia*) do you pray for this Lent?

In what ways have you, by grace and your own inner work, grown beyond your former way of life?

Closing

Conclude with one of the meditations on pages 57–58 or with a period of quiet reflection.

Bob - Stent - 3/7/12

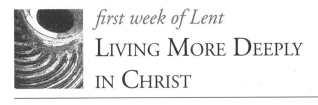

first week of Lent

LIVING MORE DEEPLY IN CHRIST

OPENING REFLECTION

FROM PSALM 31 IN *THE PSALMS, A NEW TRANSLATION*,
ARRANGED BY JOSEPH GELINEAU

> You are my hiding place, O Lord;
> You save me from distress.
> You surround me with cries of deliverance.

INTRODUCTION TO THE TEXTS

The "sackcloth and ashes" of our Lenten observance is a metaphor for our renewed intentions to transcend our habits of living that deflect our concerns for the needs of our neighbors. Lenten discipline is a personal and communal effort to reinvigorate our efforts to live beyond our shallow and too-constricted communities. A culminating moment in our common experience of Lent will be the renewing of our baptismal vows at the Easter Vigil or at Easter Sunday Mass. Our baptismal vows enjoin us to rise above the barriers that keep us hemmed in from our truer selves so that we can identify and fulfill our neighbor's needs as if they were our own.

A disciplined human being is a liberated human being. Merton urges us to train and discipline our mental and emotional faculties in order to deepen our capacities "for experience, for awareness, for understanding, for a higher kind of life. . . ." This "higher life" is lived in and for communities. This higher life provides us satisfactions more lasting than our habitual lives of consuming and spending. Lent calls us to struggle against our usual behaviors so as to live differently and more authentically "in Christ" and "in the Spirit." We discipline ourselves to live more freely in service to our neighbors.

Merton's Voice
From *Contemplation in a World of Action*

If one "trains" and disciplines one's faculties and whole being, it is in order to deepen and expand one's capacity for experience, for awareness, for understanding, for a higher kind of life, a deeper and more authentic life "in Christ" and "in the Spirit." The purpose of discipline is not only moral perfection (development of virtue for its own sake) but self-transcendence, transformation in Christ "from glory to glory, as by the Spirit of the Lord." The death and crucifixion of the old self, the routine person of self-seeking and conventionally social life, leads to the resurrection in Christ of a totally "new man" who is "one Spirit" with Christ. This new person is not just the old person in possession of a legal certificate entitling him to a reward. He is no longer the same, and his reward is precisely this transformation that makes him no longer the isolated subject of a limited reward but "one with Christ" and, in Christ, with all (p. 117).

The purpose of discipline is . . . to make us critically aware of the limitations of the very language of the spiritual life and of ideas about that life. If, on an elementary level, discipline makes us critical of sham values in social life (for example, it makes us realize experientially that happiness is not to be found in the usual rituals of consumption in an affluent society), on a higher level it reveals to us the limitations of formalistic and crude spiritual ideas. Discipline develops our critical insight and shows us the inadequacy of what we had previously accepted as valid in our religious and spiritual lives. It enables us to abandon and to discard as irrelevant certain kinds of experience which, in the past, meant a great deal to us. It makes us see that what previously served as a real "inspiration" has now become a worn-out routine and that we must go on to something else. It gives us the courage to face the risk and anguish of the break with our previous level of experience (pp. 128–129).

Another Voice
Olivier Clément, *The Roots of Christian Mysticism*

As free human beings with a capacity to "create positively," we are challenged to keep faith with the great transformation in Christ, such that we transform likewise, in the Holy Spirit, the relationship that in this world we necessarily have with material things—our genetic inheritance, psychological and social background—so that finally we transform the material things themselves.

Ascesis then is awakening from the sleepwalking of daily life. It enables the Word to clear the silt away in the depth of the soul, freeing the spring of living waters. The Word can restore to its original brightness the tarnished image of God in us, the silver coin that has rolled in the dust, but remains stamped with the king's likeness (Lk 15: 8–10). It is the Word who acts, but we have to cooperate with him, not so much by exertion of willpower as by loving attentiveness.

21

The purpose of *ascesis* is thus to divest oneself of surplus weight, of spiritual fat. It is to dissolve in the waters of baptism, in the water of tears, all the hardness of the heart, so that it may become an antenna of infinite sensitivity, infinitely vulnerable to the beauty of the world and to the sufferings of human beings, and to God who is Love, who has conquered by the wood of the Cross.

Ascesis is not obedience to some abstract categorical imperative. It frees human nature to follow its deep instinct to ascend towards God. It enables a person to pass from a state "contrary to nature" to a state "in harmony with nature," in harmony, that is, with that human (and cosmic) material united in Christ with the godhead, without separation or confusion. This is the testimony of St. Benedict, the father of Western monasticism, and of an Amma, a "mother" of the desert, St. Syncletica, whose teaching is marked by a very feminine directness, and is always close to real life. "If justice leads us to propose some mild constraint in order to correct vices and to preserve love, do not at once fly in dismay from the path of salvation, which one cannot enter except through a narrow gate. For as you advance gradually in a holy life and in faith, your heart is enlarged and you run the way of God's commandments in an ineffable sweetness of love" (Benedict of Nursia *Rule*, Prologue).

Amma Syncletica said, "Great endeavors and hard struggles await those who are converted, but afterwards inexpressible joy. If you want to light a fire, you are troubled at first by the smoke, and your eyes water. But in the end you achieve your aim. Now it is written: 'Our God is a consuming fire.' So we must light the divine fire in us with tears and struggle" (pp. 130–132).

Reflect and Dialogue

What words or sentences in these readings most resonate with your life's experiences?

In what ways do you discipline yourself in your life? Why do you discipline yourself?

For whom are you willing to make sacrifices that are apparently at the expense of your personal satisfaction?

Can you speak of areas in your own behavior that need "liberation"?

Closing

Conclude with one of the meditations on pages 57–58 or with a period of quiet reflection.

second week of Lent

A Season
for Compunction
and Tears

Opening Reflection

From Psalm 120 in *The Psalms, A New Translation,*
arranged by Joseph Gelineau

> I lift up my eyes to the mountains:
> from where shall come my help?
> My help shall come from the Lord
> who made heaven and earth.
>
> The Lord is your guard and your shade;
> at your right side he stands.
> By day the sun shall not smite you
> nor the moon in the night.

Introduction to the Texts

No matter how much "sin" is inherited from our birth
culture, no matter the quantity of passed-down sins
from the generation that bore and educated us into
this world, Lent reminds us that we are inescapably re-
sponsible for our willing commitments to what limits
our love for God and our neighbors, to what isolates us
from the natural world of our interdependence with all
beings. It is a moment of hard grace whenever we become conscious of personal failures to live in the truth
of our responsibility to our communities. The Holy
Spirit is the Spirit of Truth: It is a grace to realize that

24

we are walled-up human beings, selfish and lacking generosity.

Times of tears and regret are disguised gifts, when we see ourselves just as we are. These moments of self-recognition occasion in us a certain "dread," which Merton defines in this way:

> [Dread is] an infidelity to a personal demand of which one is at least dimly aware: the failure to meet a challenge, to fulfill a certain possibility, which demands to be met and fulfilled. The price of this failure to measure up to an existential demand of one's own life is a general sense of failure, of guilt. This guilt is real; it is not necessarily a mere neurotic anxiety. It is the sense of defection and defeat that afflicts a man who is not facing his own inner truth and is not giving back to life, to God, and to his fellow man a fair return for all that has been given him.
>
> *Contemplative Prayer, 97*

Merton's Voice
From *A Search for Solitude*

March 3, 1953. Another thing: I have discovered the Penitential Psalms.* You do not discover them until you know how much you need them. You do not know your need until you experience it. You do not experience your poverty when you tell yourself about it but when God tells you that you are poor. When God tells you of a sickness, it is because He means, at the same time, to provide a remedy. It is the Devil who tells us that we are ill and taunts us for it, reminds us of our helplessness by making us even more helpless.

In the Penitential Psalms Christ recognizes my poverty in His poverty. Merely to see myself in the psalm is a beginning of being healed. For I see myself through His grace. His grace is working; therefore, I am on my way to being healed. O the need of that healing! I walk from region to region of my soul, and I discover that I am a bombed city.

While I meditated on Psalm 6, I caught sight of an unexpected patch of green meadow along the creek of our neighbor's land. The green grass under the leafless trees, the pools of water after the storm, lifted my heart to God. He is so easy to come to when even grass and water bear witness to His mercy! "I will water my couch with tears."

I have written about the frogs singing. Now they sing again. It is another spring. Although I am ruined, I am far better off than I have ever been in my life. My ruin is my fortune (pp. 38–39).

*The Penitential Psalms are, according to the numeration of the Vulgate Latin Bible, Psalms 6, 31, 37, 50, 101, 129, and 142. Cassiodorus, a sixth-century monk, first named these the Penitential Psalms.

ANOTHER VOICE
DOUGLAS BURTON-CHRISTIE, *THE WORD IN THE DESERT*

The consciousness of the reality of judgment and of the nearness of the "end time" inspired among the desert fathers a sensitive understanding of the heart's movement toward renewal, which they called *penthos* or compunction. The monks' awareness and sorrow for their faults and the need for and experience of forgiveness sometimes pierced the heart so deeply that tears burst forth. Thus *penthos* was sometimes called "the gift of tears." It involved a "double movement" of the heart: "*penthos* or compunction is the way believers accept both judgment and mercy simultaneously." It was a transforming experience. Through the piercing of the heart, the old experience of the world was washed away and a new one emerged. In this way, one could begin again—or take up again—the path toward God. Scripture was one of the places the monks looked to learn about *penthos*. There they found descriptions and examples of deep repentance which they attempted to emulate in their own lives. . . . As Luciana Mortari suggests, "*Penthos* is seen as an essential, not a marginal aspect part of the fulcrum of the spiritual life.". . .

Penthos, like the call to repentance in the gospels, demanded a fundamental reorientation of one's entire being, so that one would be prepared to enter the world of the kingdom of God. As such, acquiring the spirit of *penthos* involved dying to oneself, at least to those inner habits and addictions which prevented a single-minded devotion to God (p. 186).

Reflect and Dialogue

What words or sentences in these readings most resonate with your life's experiences?

What moments in your life were moments of conversion, when you wanted to love God more deeply?

When in your life have you truly felt "compunction," knowing you were failing someone or a call to responsibility?

At what time in your life could you, too, have said with Merton that "My ruin is my fortune"?

Closing

Conclude with one of the meditations on pages 57–58 or with a period of quiet reflection.

third week of Lent

IN ALL THINGS, ALWAYS SEEKING GOD

OPENING REFLECTION

FROM PSALM 94 IN *THE PSALMS, A NEW TRANSLATION,*
ARRANGED BY JOSEPH GELINEAU

> Come, ring out our joy to the Lord;
> hail the rock who saves us.
> Let us come before him, giving thanks,
> with songs let us hail the Lord.
>
> Come in; let us bow and bend low;
> let us kneel before the God who made us
> for he is our God and we
> the people who belong to his pasture,
> the flock that is led by his hand.
>
> O that today you would listen to his voice!
> Harden not your hearts as at Meribah,
> as on that day at Massah in the desert
> when your fathers put me to the test;
> when they tried me, though they saw my work.

INTRODUCTION TO THE TEXTS

Through Christ's revelation to us, we understand God's will to be that we realize we are one body, one humankind enfleshed together on our precarious journey through life. The pinnacle of life in Christ is the full realization of our baptismal vows to adhere to God

29

through all of life's ten thousand things. Hard as it is for us to learn the simple lesson, we only become saints by surrendering in courage to the ordinary challenges presented to us every day.

Each family of us is a little church. The tasks of service in front of our noses are God's will for us; they are our part in building up the family of humankind. If you drive a taxi or asphalt a road, if you teach a child to dance or one young woman to sing, you take part in building the kingdom where God is for all.

Christ is most intimate to us when we recognize Christ in those with whom we live most intimately every day, in those with whom every day we share the sacrament of time. In our intercessory prayers for our intimates, for our extended families, for the people we work with, for the guys who collect the garbage, we are literally forming a web of truth, goodness, and beauty through which we are all becoming One Body in Christ. Our prayers of intercession weave the web of the Church into deeper communion—a unity the early Church called *koinonia*—until the Lord comes. We are each Web sites for the Church and we are posting the Word of God to the world every day.

Merton's Voice
From *Seasons of Celebration*

We must in all things seek God. But we do not seek Him the way we seek a lost object, a "thing." He is present to us in our heart, our personal subjectivity, and to seek Him is to recognize this fact. Yet we cannot be aware of it as a reality unless He reveals His presence to us. He does not reveal Himself simply in our heart. He reveals Himself to us through one another. He reveals Himself to us in the Church, in the community of believers, in the *koinonia* of those who trust Him and love Him.

Seeking God is not just an operation of the intellect, or even a contemplative illumination of the mind. We seek God by striving to surrender ourselves to Him whom we do not see, but Who is in all things and through all things and above all things.

We seek God by surrendering ourselves to His will. But His will is not just a matter of blind decrees and laws external to ourselves. It is the law of love which is implanted in every nature, and the revelation of spiritual love in personal freedom. The fruit of this love is the restoration of all things in Christ, the union of all beings with God, through man, by the exercise of man's freedom.

Man's freedom is therefore the instrument of divine redemption and reconciliation. This work of reconciliation requires the formation of a living body of men who are united by the Spirit of God. God's work is to form a living mystical body, which will be His Son, the One Christ, Head and Members, in which all the members share One Spirit, One Sonship, and are "One in Christ."

For this, each member must undergo a transformation by the Holy Spirit. Each must undergo a renewal in the depths of his being. . . .

This renewal is to be seen from many points of view: as renunciation, as pardon, as conversion, as "justification," as self-surrender, as thanksgiving, "*eucharistia*." The word "love" in the sense of *Agape* perfectly covers and includes them all (pp. 224–225).

ANOTHER VOICE
ALEXANDER SCHMEMANN, "THE MISSION OF ORTHODOXY"

[In this excerpt Schmemann proposes a new form of monasticism for laypersons, without celibacy and without "the desert," but with three specific vows.]

The first vow is to keep a certain well-defined spiritual discipline of life, and this means *a rule of prayer*; an effort to maintain a level of personal contact with God, what the Fathers call the "inner memory of Him." It is very fashionable today to discuss spirituality and to read books about it. But whatever the degree of our theoretical knowledge about spirituality, it must begin with a simple and humble decision, an effort and—what is most difficult—regularity. Nothing indeed is more dangerous than pseudo-spirituality, whose unmistakable signs are self-righteousness, pride, readiness to measure other's people's spirituality, and emotionalism. What the world needs now is a generation of men and women not only speaking about Christianity, but also living it. Early monasticism was, first of all, a rule of prayer. It is precisely a rule we need, one that could be practiced and followed by all and not only by some. For indeed what you say is less and less important today. [People] are moved only by what you are, and this means the total impact of your personality, of your personal experience, commitment, and dedication. . . .

Perhaps without noticing it, we live in a climate of radical individualism. Each one tailors for himself his own kind of "Orthodoxy," his own ideal of the Church, his own style of life. And yet, the whole literature of spirituality emphasizes *obedience* as the condition of all spiritual progress. What I mean, however, is something very practical . . . obedience to the movement of life itself . . . obedience in small things, humble chores, the unromantic routine of work . . . the antithesis not of disobedience, but of hysterical individualism: "I" feel, "I" don't feel. Stop "feeling" and do.

The third vow, *acceptance*, which could be described, in terms of one spiritual author [St. Bernard of Clairvaux], as "digging one's own well." So many people want to do anything except precisely what God wants them to do, for to accept this, and perhaps even to discern it, is one of the greatest spiritual difficulties. It is very significant that ascetical literature is full of warnings against changing places, against leaving monasteries for other and "better" ones, against the spirit of unrest, that constant search for the best possible conditions. Again, what we need today is to relate to the Church and to Christ our lives, our professions, and the unique combination of factors which God gives us as our examination and which we alone pass or fail. . . . We must think in terms of a remnant, of a movement, of service. We must begin with ourselves, if we are to be of service to the Church. When God gives something, a talent, He wants us to invest it. He wants us to serve. There is no other way of following Christ (pp. 21–23).

Reflect and Dialogue

What words or sentences in these readings most resonate with your life's experiences?

By what means does God most clearly reveal His presence to you?

What is your personal rule of prayer? How do you pray regularly?

How do you seek God's will in your life and for the persons with whom you are living?

Closing

Conclude with one of the meditations on pages 57–58 or with a period of quiet reflection.

3|26

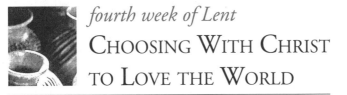

fourth week of Lent

Choosing With Christ to Love the World

Opening Reflection

FROM PSALM 22 IN *THE PSALMS, A NEW TRANSLATION*, ARRANGED BY JOSEPH GELINEAU

The Lord is my shepherd;
there is nothing I shall want.
Fresh and green are the pastures
where he gives me repose,
near restful waters he leads me,
To revive my drooping spirit

He guides me along the right path;
he is true to his name.
If I should walk in the valley of darkness
no evil shall I fear.
You are there with your crook and your staff;
With these you give me comfort.

Introduction to the Texts

We stand united to one another on the same ground of God's love. The Holy Spirit supports us as we co-create the development of that portion of the world entrusted to each of us. We are co-producers in the formation of our communal identities. We affect together all that is ongoing within the matrix of nature's and history's evolutions. Within the trinity of our relationships to our own self-formation, to the formation of community with our neighbors, and to the natural order of things, we are sustained by the Source of all these relationships, who underwrites all beings through space and time. The Source of all our relationships, for Christians who believe and trust in God, is the personal *Logos*, the ordering Word, the Christ who is Lord and who energizes our becoming one with everything in what Merton called "that hidden ground of love for which there can be no explanations" (*The Hidden Ground of Love*, p. 115).

God has revealed God's Self as Love and, Interrelationship. Lent is a special season to acknowledge and live out our share in the divine intercommunion of all beings by our adhering more intimately to Christ. Our vocation is to love the world, as the Father loved the world by choosing his Son to transform our natures for Himself. Our vocation is to help redeem the world, with humility and responsibility, with the energies of the Holy Spirit assisting us to make all things in our world gradually new.

MERTON'S VOICE
FROM *LORETTO AND GETHSEMANI*

There is nothing more positive, more creative than the faith by which the Creator of all dwells and acts in our hearts. And yet, as we know from our own past history, the ideal of "keeping the faith" can sometimes dwindle into something very negative, resentful, and obtuse: a mere "no" to everything that we do not agree with. We can no longer afford to barricade ourselves in our Catholic environment and regard it as a little smug fortress of security in a world of pagans. Now most of all we are obliged by our faith and by our love

36

of truth to commit ourselves humbly and completely not only to the message of Christ but also to all that is valid in human culture and civilization: for this too is His by right. Not only is it something we must salvage for Him, but more, it is not unconnected with our own salvation. If the Lord of all took flesh and sanctified nature, restoring it to the Father by His resurrection, we too have our work to do in extending the power of the resurrection to the whole world of our time by our prayer, our thought, our work and our whole life. Nothing so effectively prevents this as the division, the discontinuity of spiritual lives that place God and prayer in one compartment, work and apostolate in another, as if prayer and work were somehow opposed. The Cross is the sign of contradiction, but also and above all a sign of reconciliation. It reminds us of the contradictions within ourselves, and within our society, only in order to resolve them all in unity in love of the Savior. Unity is a sign of strength and spiritual health. This unity in Christ is the true secret of our Christian and religious vocations, whether our lives be active or contemplative.

False unity is the work of force. It is violently imposed on divided entities which stubbornly refuse to be one. True unity is the work of love. It is the free union of beings that spontaneously seek to be one in the truth, preserving and elevating their separate selves by self-transcendence. True unity admits the presence of obstacles, and of divisions, in order to overcome both by humility and sacrifice.

Here, in facing contradiction, we can hope for grace from God that will produce a unity and a peace "which the world cannot give"(p. 1).

would we strive to be "better people" w/o the gospel

37

Another Voice
Mother Teresa of Calcutta, *One Heart Full of Love*

We should gather to give thanks to God for what he has done in us, with us, through us. We thank him for having used you and us to be his love and mercy. God is still love, and he still loves the world. We believe that God so loved the world that he gave his only begotten Son. And God so loves the world today that he gives you and me to love the world, so that we may be his love and his mercy. What a beautiful thought and conviction for us, that we can be that love and mercy right in our homes, above all. Then we can be that love and mercy for our next-door neighbors and for our neighbors down the street.

But do we know our neighbors? Do we know the poor in our neighborhood? It's easier for us to talk and talk about the poor in far-away places. We are often surrounded by the sick and the abandoned. We are often among people who are despised, outcast, and depressed. We have many elderly whom we don't even know. At times, we don't even have the time to smile at these people.

As Jesus' co-workers, one thing we have to learn is to sow joy. We don't need bombs or weapons to bring peace to the world. We need that love and compassion that we ask for every day. We need a truly compassionate love—a compassion and love that bring joy and peace. The world is hungry for God. . . .

The work each one of you carries out in your families, for those you love, is an expression of our love for God. Love starts at home. For your love to be real, it cannot waver at home (pp. 90–91).

Reflect and Dialogue

What words or sentences in these readings most resonate with your life's experiences?

How are you extending the power of Christ's resurrection to the world?

On the basis of how you actually live your life, how broad and extended is your conception of the world?

How would you answer Mother Teresa's questions: "Do you know your neighbors? Do you know the poor of your neighborhood?"

Closing

Conclude with one of the meditations on pages 57–58 or with a period of quiet reflection.

fifth week of Lent
IN THE SERVICE OF PEACE THROUGH HUMILITY AND PRAYER

OPENING REFLECTION

FROM PSALM 129 IN *THE PSALMS, A NEW TRANSLATION*, ARRANGED BY JOSEPH GELINEAU

> Out of the depths I cry to you, O Lord,
> Lord, hear my voice!
> O let your ears be attentive
> to the voice of my pleading.
>
> My soul is waiting for the Lord,
> I count on his word.
> My soul is longing for the Lord
> more than watchmen for daybreak.
>
> Because with the Lord there is mercy
> and fullness of redemption,
> Israel indeed he will redeem
> from all its iniquity.

INTRODUCTION TO THE TEXTS

Life and Death are identical twin sisters born within every human being. We are all kin as we travel the uneven roads of our common journey through life. Yet being kindred, why are we so unkind to one another? Why do we find it so hard to see each other's dilemmas as being identical to our own? Why do we so often accept unkindness as the order of relations among us? For us to live unkindly with one another is to live unnaturally.

How do we learn to live kindly in an unkind world? Humility teaches us kindness. Humility prevents our taking the first places at life's banquet, prevents our excessive consumption of resources while sisters and brothers on other continents or just down the street cannot feed their children. Humility helps us step down from the pedestal of individual destinies to share life with the crowd. Humility helps us see how easy it is to lose everything we hold dear in an instant: our houses, our status, our families, our very selves lost in the distractions of the ten thousand things that keep us from realizing our kindness with one another.

Lent is an occasion for us to reorder our priorities, to attend to the least privileged first, to allow the lame to lead us in procession through life by their slower pace and with rhythms that appreciate how we must all proceed together carefully or suffer soul-death alone.

MERTON'S VOICE
FROM *THE MONASTIC JOURNEY*

We prescribe for one another remedies that will bring us peace of mind, and we are still devoured by anxiety. We evolve plans for disarmament and for the peace of nations, and our plans only change the manner and method of aggression. The rich have everything they want except happiness, and the poor are sacrificed to the unhappiness of the rich. Dictatorships use their secret police to crush millions of men under an intolerable burden of lies, injustice, and tyranny, and those who live in democracies have forgotten how to make good use of their liberty. For liberty is a thing of the spirit, and we are no longer able to live for anything but our bodies. How can we find peace, true peace, if we forget that we are not machines for making money and spending money, but spiritual beings, sons and daughters of the Most High God?

Yet there *is* peace in the world. Where is it to be found? In the hearts of men and women who are wise because they are humble—humble enough to be at peace in the midst of anguish, to accept conflict and insecurity and overcome it with love, because they realize who they are, and therefore possess the freedom that is their true heritage. These are the children of God. We all know them. We do not have to go to monasteries to find them. They are everywhere. They may not spend their time talking about peace, or about God, or about Christ our Lord, but they know peace and they know God, and they have found Christ in the midst of battle. They have surrendered their minds and their wills to the call of Christ, and in Him they have found reality. . . .

The peace which Christ brings is not a formula for individual escape, nor for egotistical self-fulfillment. There can be no peace in the heart of the man who seeks peace for himself alone. To find true peace, peace in Christ, we must desire others to have peace as well as ourselves, and we must be willing to sacrifice something of our own peace and happiness in order that others may have peace, and that others may be happy. . . .

. . . Peace does not mean the suppression of all differences, but their coexistence and fruitful collaboration. Peace does not consist in one man, one party, one nation, crushing and dominating everyone else. Peace exists where men who have the power to be enemies are, instead, friends by reason of the sacrifices they have made in order to meet one another on a higher level, where the differences between them are no longer a source of conflict (pp. 40–41).

ANOTHER VOICE
JAMES FINLEY, *MERTON'S PALACE OF NOWHERE*

Merton once told me that prayer must make us more sensitive to the plight of others. He said, "As long as one person suffers, you suffer, too. It must be so or your prayer is of little value." Saint Paul's "I fill up what is lacking in the suffering of Christ" is closely attuned to these words of Merton. It is so easy to misinterpret talk of ecstasy, of self beyond self, mystical union, or such similar expressions as implying a distance between our inner self and the daily simple problems of others. In a sense this is so. There is a distance proper to prayer. We go off and pray in secret. We go off alone. We go off, leaving even ourselves as we normally conceive of ourselves. But this distance is for the sake of union. Solitude, if it is genuine, brings us to a most profound communion with others in their deepest reality grounded in God. . . .

If Christian service is authentic, it gradually deepens our desire to see directly the face of God reflected in the faces of our brothers and sisters. . . .

Christ served many people in many ways. Yet his greatest service, his greatest sign of power this side of death, was his death itself. Helplessly nailed to the cross, he saved us by handing himself over to the Father. Prayer is a vital expression of our share in this handing over, this deliverance, this passing over from death to life. Surely, central to the gospel is the truth that Christ came not only to unite us to one another but to take us in the Spirit to the Father. In prayer is found the ground of service, the ultimate why behind the truth that to help another is to draw closer to Christ (pp. 66–67).

REFLECT AND DIALOGUE

What words or sentences in these readings most reso-nate with your life's experiences?

What role does "humility" play in your life?

Who have been peacemakers in your life? For whom are you a peacemaker?

Has your way of praying changed during this season of Lent? How?

CLOSING

Conclude with one of the meditations on pages 57–58 or with a period of quiet reflection.

Holy Week

RETURNING TO THE SOURCE OF OUR UNITY IN CHRIST

OPENING REFLECTION

FROM PSALM 137 IN *THE PSALMS, A NEW TRANSLATION,* ARRANGED BY JOSEPH GELINEAU

> I thank you, Lord, with all my heart,
> you have heard the words of my mouth.
> In the presence of the angels I will bless you.
> I will adore before your holy temple.
>
> I thank you for your faithfulness and love
> which excel all we ever knew of you.
> On the day I called, you answered;
> you increased the strength of my soul.
>
> All earth's kings shall thank you
> when they hear the words of your mouth.
> They shall sing of the Lord's way:
> "How great is the glory of the Lord!"

INTRODUCTION TO THE TEXTS

Today Christ washes the feet of his disciples. Today Christ breaks the bread and blesses the cup and gives them to his disciples, requesting that they eat and drink in communion with his very life for them. Today Christ suffers an agony of submission to Love's requests in the Garden of Gethsemani. Today Christ is lifted up and draws all things to Himself. Today Christ is buried in the tomb. Today Christ breaks the bonds of hell and draws Adam and Eve, the prophets, the kings, Abraham and Sarah, and John the Baptist upward toward the Father to that Kingdom prepared for them from the beginning of the world.

These sacred days are the holiest of Christian feasts. We are lifted up by Christ to consider the end for which the world was created. In the words of Christ's own formulation, this is our "return to the Father." Plunging together into the depths of mysteries that we can only comprehend by faith and love for Christ, we rise through these sacred days into new being, into a renewed community washed again in the Lamb's blood. These sacred days anoint us as messengers of joy and gratitude to the world. Each of us today becomes a bearer of the Lord's Gospel by our service and hospitality to all.

"Our glory and our hope: we are the Body of Christ," Merton wrote in *Conjectures of A Guilty Bystander*. "Christ loves and espouses us as His own flesh. Isn't that enough for us? But we do not really believe it. No! Be content, be content. We are the Body of Christ! We have found Him because He has sought us. God has come to take up His abode in us, in sinners. There is nothing further to look for except to turn to Him completely, where He is already present. Be quiet and see that He is God" (p. 23).

MERTON'S VOICE
FROM *CONJECTURES OF A GUILTY BYSTANDER*

One thing above all is important: the "return to the Father."

47

The Son came into the world and died for us, rose and ascended to the Father; sent us His Spirit, that in Him and with Him we might return to the Father.

That we might pass clean out of the midst of all that is transitory and inconclusive, return to the Immense, the Primordial, the Source, the Unknown, to Him Who loves and knows, to the Silent, to the Merciful, to the Holy, to Him Who is All.

To seek anything, to be concerned with anything but this is only madness and sickness, for this is the whole meaning and heart of all existence, and in this all the affairs of life, all the needs of the world and of men, take on their right significance: All point to this one great return to the Source.

All goals that are not ultimate, all "ends of the line" that we can see and plan as "ends," are simply absurd, because they do not even begin. The "return" is the end beyond all ends and the beginning of beginnings. . . .

Our destiny is to go beyond everything, to leave everything, to press forward to the End and find in the End our Beginning, the ever-new Beginning that has no end; to obey Him on the way, in order to reach Him in whom I have begun, who is the key and the end—because He is the Beginning (pp. 171–172).

ANOTHER VOICE
SAINT PAUL, *COLOSSIANS 1:15–23*

He is the image of the invisible God, the firstborn of all creation; for in him all things in heaven and on earth were created, things visible and invisible, whether thrones or dominions or rulers or powers—all things have been created through him and for him. He himself is before all things, and in him all things hold together. He is the head of the body, the church; he is the beginning, the firstborn from the dead, so that he might come to have first place in everything. For in him all the fullness of God was pleased to dwell, and through him God was pleased to reconcile to himself all things, whether on earth or in heaven, by making peace through the blood of his cross.

And you who were once estranged and hostile in mind, doing evil deeds, he has now reconciled—in his fleshly body through death, so as to present you holy and blameless and irreproachable before him— provided that you continue securely established and steadfast in the faith, without shifting from the hope promised by the gospel that you heard, which has been proclaimed to every creature under heaven. I, Paul, became a servant of this gospel.

Reflect and Dialogue

What words or sentences in these readings most resonate with your life's experiences?

What metaphors would you use to describe your life's progress?

What do you tell others when they ask you, "What should human beings be living for?"

Saint Paul tells us who Christ was for him. Who is Christ for you?

Closing

Conclude with one of the meditations on pages 57–58 or with a period of quiet reflection.

the Resurrection of the Lord
LIBERATED TO REDEEM
THE WORLD

OPENING REFLECTION

FROM PSALM 137 IN *THE PSALMS, A NEW TRANSLATION*, ARRANGED BY JOSEPH GELINEAU

> Alleluia!
> O give thanks to the Lord for he is good,
> for his love endures forever.
> Give thanks to the God of gods,
> for his love endures forever.
> Give thanks to the Lord of lords,
> for his love endures forever.

INTRODUCTION TO THE TEXTS

Nothing in Jesus is alien to us. The "Firstborn of all creation" ate and drank with sinners. He healed the sick. He raised the dead to life. He was a sign of compassion. He was the kingdom of the Father's love for humankind being inaugurated. We, his disciples who believe and love Him, continue His mission to establish the kingdom of our unity with the Father over that portion of life given to us, the persons given to us, the tasks our daily lives require us to do. Nothing human is alien to Jesus, like us in all things but sin.

After three days in the tomb, Lazarus woke from death at the call of his beloved friend Jesus, "Lazarus, rise up and come out!" Did his eyes look first for the face of Jesus, or did they focus on his sisters, Martha and Mary? The gospel tells us that Jesus left the scene quickly since he had to be about his Father's business. He left Martha and Mary to peel away their brother's burial shroud and make him supper. Until the Lord comes again, we are left in each other's arms, not only to receive the nourishment we need, but also to taste a portion of that Love that will one day raise us all together from the dead.

We are all one kind, one human kind: we must recognize ourselves as kin or we will not be well. Jesus' identification with all of us, his kindness to all persons is our cure. Kindness is the Lord's blessing to be prayed for every day until His light opens a new vista for our eyes and everywhere we look we can see kin, our own kind. Though we remain a community of sinners, let us imitate the Lord's kindness. Even in the middle of all that fails us and in full view of Sorrow's face, may we live for Christ's coming again, may we live to see the paradise of our hidden kindness with everything the Father created revealed at last. Come, Lord Jesus!

Merton's Voice
From *He Is Risen*

"He has risen, he is not here . . . he is going before you to Galilee" (Mk 16:6–7).

Christ is risen, Christ lives. Christ is the Lord of the living and the dead. He is the Lord of history.

Christ is the Lord of a history that moves. He not only holds the beginning and the end in his hands, but he is in history with us, walking ahead of us to where we are going. He is not always in the same place. . . .

Christ lives in us and leads us, through mutual encounter and commitment, into a new future which we build together for one another. That future is called the Kingdom of God. The Kingdom is already established; the Kingdom is a present reality. But there is still work to be done. Christ calls us to work together in building his Kingdom. We cooperate with him in bringing it to perfection.

Such is the timeless message of the Church not only on Easter Sunday but every day of the year and every year until the world's end. The dynamism of the Easter mystery is at the heart of the Christian faith. It is the life of the Church. The Resurrection is not a doctrine we try to prove or a problem we argue about: It is the life and action of Christ himself in us by his Holy Spirit. . . .

True encounter with Christ liberates something in us, a power that we did not know we had, a hope, a capacity for life, resilience, an ability to bounce back when we thought we were completely defeated, a capacity to grow and change, a power of creative transformation.

The risen life is not easy; it is also a dying life. The presence of the Resurrection in our lives means the presence of the Cross, for we do not rise with Christ unless we also die with him. It is by the Cross that we enter the dynamism of creative transformation, the dynamism of resurrection and renewal, the dynamism of love (pp. 5–13).

ANOTHER VOICE
PAUL EVDOKIMOV, *THE SACRAMENT OF LOVE*

Each layperson participates in the unique priesthood of Christ by his sanctified being. Every baptized person is sealed with the gifts, anointed by the Holy Spirit in his very essence and is the priest of his own existence, offering in sacrifice the whole of his life and existence. This is the consecration of one's whole life to the ministry of the laity, a ministry that is essentially ecclesial, of the Church. The eschatological emphasis of the prayer [of tonsure] reinforces this meaning: "May he/she give glory and have all the days of his/her life the vision of the joys of Jerusalem." Thus every instant of time is directed to the eschatological dimension. Every act and word is in the service of the King. In the rite of tonsure, every baptized person is a monk of interiorized monasticism, subject to all the requirements of the Gospel. In addition to those commissioned as missionaries by the Church, every baptized and confirmed person is an "apostolic being," each in his or her own way. It is by my whole being and life, that I am called to give constant witness. The laity forms an ecclesial dimension that is, at one and the same time, of the world and of the Church. By the simple presence in the world of "sanctified beings," of "priests" in their very substance, of "dwelling places of the Trinity," the universal priesthood of the laity bears the power of the sacred in the world, celebrating the liturgy of the entire cosmos therein. Beyond the church walls, lay people continue the liturgy of the Church. By their active presence, they introduce into society and all human relationships the truth of the dogmas they live, thus dislodging the evil and profane elements of the world. Here is a magnificent definition . . . by one's whole being, by one's whole existence, to become a living theology—theophanic—the luminous place of the *Parousia*, God's coming again (p. 92).

Reflect and Dialogue

What words or sentences in these readings most resonate with your life's experiences?

What does renewing your baptismal promises on Holy Saturday or Easter Sunday mean to you?

In what ways could you view your life's progress as a "creative transformation"?

What significant changes have you experienced during this season of Lent?

Closing

Conclude with one of the meditations on pages 57–58 or with a period of quiet reflection.

Concluding Meditations

A.

My Lord God, I have no idea where I am going. I do not see the road ahead of me. I cannot know for certain where it will end. Nor do I really know myself, and the fact that I think I am following your will does not mean that I am actually doing so. But I believe that the desire to please you does in fact please you. And I hope I have that desire in all that I am doing. I hope that I will never do anything apart from that desire. And I know that if I do this you will lead me by the right road though I may know nothing about it. Therefore I will trust you always though I may seem to be lost in the shadow of death. I will not fear, for you are ever with me, and you will never leave me to face my perils alone.

Thomas Merton
Thoughts in Solitude, p. 83

B.

My true personality will be fulfilled in the Mystical Christ in this one way above all, that through me Christ and His Spirit will be able to love you and all men and God the Father in a way that would be possible in no one else.

Love comes out of God and gathers us to God in order to pour itself back into God through all of us and bring us all back to Him on the tide of His own infinite mercy.

So we all become doors and windows through which God shines back into His own house.

When the Love of God is in me, God is able to love you through me and you are able to love God through me. If my soul were closed to that love, God's love for you and your love for God and God's love for Himself in you and in me, would be denied the particular expression which it finds through me and no others.

Because God's love is in me, it can come to you from a different and special direction that would be closed if He did not live in me, and because His love is in you, it can come to me from a quarter from which it would not otherwise come. And because it is in both of us, God has greater glory. His love is expressed in two more ways in which it would not otherwise be expressed; that is, in two more joys that could not exist without Him.

Thomas Merton
New Seeds of Contemplation, p. 67

C.

The grace of Easter is a great silence, an immense tranquility and a clean taste in your soul. It is the taste of heaven, but not the heaven of some wild exaltation. The Easter vision is not riot and drunkenness of spirit, but a discovery of order above all order—a discovery of God and of all things in Him. This is a wine without intoxication, a joy that has no poison in it. It is life without death. Tasting it for a moment, we are briefly able to see and love all things according to their truth, to possess them in their substance hidden in God, beyond all sense. For desire clings to the vesture and accident of things, but charity possess them in the simple depths of God.

Thomas Merton
The Sign of Jonas, pp. 297–298

Sources

The readings from the Psalms are from *The Psalms: A New Translation*. Arranged by Joseph Gelineau. New York/Mahwah: Paulist Press, 1966. Gelineau numbered the Psalms according to the numeration of the Vulgate Latin Bible.

From Thomas Merton:

Conjectures of A Guilty Bystander. New York: Doubleday, 1966.

Contemplation in a World of Action. New York: Doubleday, 1971.

Contemplative Prayer. New York: Doubleday, 1969.

He Is Risen. Niles, IL: Argus Communications, 1975.

The Hidden Ground of Love. William H. Shannon, ed. New York: Farrar, Straus & Giroux, 1985.

"Loretto and Gethsemani." Trappist, KY: Abbey of Gethsemani, 1962.

The Monastic Journey. Brother Patrick Hart, ed. Kalamazoo, MI: Cistercian Publications, 1992.

New Seeds of Contemplation. New York: New Directions, 1962.

Seasons of Celebration. New York: Farrar, Straus & Giroux, 1965.

A Search for Solitude: Journals, vol. 3. Patrick Hart, ed. San Francisco: HarperSanFrancisco, 1996.

The Sign of Jonas. New York: Harcourt, Brace and Company, 1953.

Thoughts in Solitude. New York: Farrar, Straus & Cudahy, 1958.

Other Voices:

Burton-Christie, Douglas. *The Word in the Desert: Scripture and the Quest for Holiness in Early Monasticism.* New York: Oxford University Press, 1993.

Clément, Olivier. *The Roots of Christian Mysticism.* Hyde Park, NY: New City Press, 1993.

Evdokimov, Paul. *The Sacrament of Love: The Nuptial Mystery in the Light of the Orthodox Tradition.* Anthony P. Gythiel, trans. Crestwood, NY: St. Vladimir Press, 1997. Originally published as *Sacrement de l'amour* (Paris, 1977). The selected passage is edited by Michael Plekon in *Living Icons: Persons of Faith in the Eastern Church.* Notre Dame, IN: University of Notre Dame Press, 2002.

Finley, James. *Merton's Palace of Nowhere.* Notre Dame, IN: Ave Maria Press, 1978.

Funk, Margaret Mary, O.S.B. *Humility Matters.* New York: Continuum, 2005.

Mother Teresa. *One Heart Full of Love.* José Luis González-Balado, ed. Ann Arbor, MI: Servant Publications, 1988.

Schmemann, Alexander. "The Mission of Orthodoxy," *Concern 3* (1968) reprinted by Conciliar Press, 1989, 1994.

other voices

BIOGRAPHICAL SKETCHES

Douglas Burton-Christie is an associate professor of theological studies and graduate director for the Department of Theological Studies at Loyola Marymount University. He publishes on ancient Christian monasticism and the relationship between spirituality and the natural world. He is the founding editor of *Spiritus: A Journal of Christian Spirituality*.

Olivier Clément is a French Orthodox theologian who has taught at the Saint Sergius Institute in Paris. In addition to *The Roots of Christian Mysticism*, he has authored many other books, including *On Human Being: Spiritual Anthropology*.

Paul Evdokimov (1902–1970) was an Orthodox theologian who taught at the Saint Sergius Institute in Paris. Many of his books resonate with the "priesthood of the laity," including *The Three Ages of the Spiritual Life*, *Woman and the Salvation of the World*, and *The Sacrament of Love*—this last a theology of Christian marriage.

James Finley is a clinical psychologist in private practice and a popular retreat leader. His book, *Merton's Palace of Nowhere*, has been in print for over twenty-five years. He also authored *The Contemplative Heart*.

Mary Margaret Funk, O.S.B., served as executive director of Monastic Interreligious Dialogue from 1994–2004. In addition to *Humility Matters*, she authored *Thoughts Matter* and *Tools Matter*, a trilogy that traces the patterns of Christian transformation into a life lived for God, neighbor, and the world according to the ancient teachers who followed Christ and whose perennial wisdom of experience guides the Church today.

Mother Teresa, born Agnes Goxha Bojaxhiu (1910–1997), was a Roman Catholic nun who founded the Missionaries of Charity in Calcutta, India in 1950. She was internationally recognized for her work with the dying, poor, and helpless. She won the Nobel Peace Prize in 1979. Pope John Paul II officially beatified her under the name Blessed Teresa of Calcutta in 2003.

Alexander Schmemann (1921–1983) was a prominent Orthodox Christian priest, teacher, and writer. He was dean of St. Vladimir's Orthodox Theological Seminary from 1961 until his death. He wrote many books of liturgical theology including *For the Life of the World: Sacraments and Orthodoxy* (1970) and *The Eucharist: Sacrament of the Kingdom* (1988).

about

THE EDITORS

The Merton Institute for Contemplative Living is dedicated to personal spiritual transformation through raising awareness of Merton's spiritual insights and contemplative practices. Its purpose is to promote his vision for a just and peaceful world.

Robert G. Toth has served as the executive director of The Merton Institute for Contemplative Living since 1998. He is the editor of the *Contemplation and Action* newsletter and wrote the foreword to *Thomas Merton: An Introduction* by William H. Shannon.

Jonathan Montaldo is resident director of Bethany Spring, the Merton Institute Retreat Center one mile from the Abbey of Gethsemani, and is associate director of the Merton Institute for Contemplative Living. He is a former director of the Thomas Merton Center at Bellarmine University and a past president of the International Thomas Merton Society. Montaldo edited *Entering the Silence*, Journal Volume 2 (1996) and *The Intimate Merton* with Brother Patrick Hart (1999). He also published *Dialogues with Silence* (2001); *Merton & Hesychasm* (2003); *A Year with Thomas Merton* (2005); *Lent & Easter Wisdom* from Thomas Merton (2007); *Thomas Merton: In My Own Words* (2007); and *Choosing to Love the World: Thomas Merton on Contemplation* (2008).